Minute Help Guides Presents:

A Newbies Guide to PowerPoint 2013 RT

Minute Help Guides

Minute Help Press

www.minutehelp.com

Cover Image © Picture-Factory - Fotolia.com.jpg

Table of Contents

INTRODUCTION 3

PART ONE: GETTING STARTED WITH POWERPOINT RT 2013 4

    CHAPTER 1: FIRST THINGS FIRST - SUPPORTED DEVICES, KEYBOARD COVERS, AND OTHER ACCESSORIES 5

    CHAPTER 2: MORE THAN A SLIDESHOW - A QUICK POWERPOINT PRIMER 8

    CHAPTER 3: UPDATING/FINALIZING OFFICE RT 11

    CHAPTER 4: NAVIGATING POWERPOINT 2013 RT - THE BASICS 16

PART TWO: USING POWERPOINT 2013 RT 20

    CHAPTER 1: THE RIBBON MENU - EASIER THAN IT LOOKS 21

    CHAPTER 2: CREATING A PRESENTATION 23

    CHAPTER 3: SMARTART AND PHOTOS 29

    CHAPTER 4: WORKING WITH AUDIO AND VIDEO 33

    CHAPTER 5: TRANSITIONS AND ANIMATIONS 37

PART THREE: GETTING MORE OUT OF POWERPOINT 2013 RT 39

    CHAPTER 1: RECORDING AND EXPORTING 41

    CHAPTER 2: SHARING AND PRESENTING 44

    CHAPTER 3: PRESENTING, PROJECTORS AND SECONDARY DISPLAYS 46

    CHAPTER 4: MAKING BETTER POWERPOINT PRESENTATIONS 49

CONCLUSION 51

ABOUT MINUTE HELP PRESS 52

Introduction

PowerPoint is everywhere. From the company-wide sales meeting to the high school chemistry class, few people have managed to avoid contact with the world's most popular presentation software. Since the 1990 introduction of PowerPoint as an integral part of the Microsoft Office suite, this little piece of software ingenuity has single-handedly destroyed the cumbersome slide projector and ushered in the very concept of the presentation into the 21st century.

Though many companies have tried to compete with PowerPoint, none have ever succeeded in any significant way. In fact, PowerPoint retains a 95 percent share of the presentation software market to this very day. They've managed this feat by becoming the rarest kind of software: simple, yet amazingly powerful. PowerPoint is currently being used by virtually anyone who needs to present an idea to a group of people. From the CEO of the largest corporation right down to your friendly local Girl Scout troop, millions of people depend on PowerPoint to help them get their ideas across.

With the release of Office 2013 RT, the PowerPoint interface has been optimized and customized for tablet PCs, giving you all of the power of this incredible program while letting you create your presentation masterpieces from anywhere you please.

This guide will take you through the basics of PowerPoint RT. We'll teach you what you need to know to get started, everything from creating and saving your presentations (with SkyDrive) to turning your finished masterpieces into stand-alone files or even videos. Whether you've been using PowerPoint for years, or you're still futzing around with a slide projector in your basement, we'll not only show you how to get things done with PowerPoint, we'll have fun doing it!

At a glance, PowerPoint RT looks like an incredibly complex program. It *can* be, but it definitely doesn't *have* to be. This guide will teach you what you need to know to get to work *right now*. We'll leave the fluff and head scratching for people with time to waste.

Ready to get started? Let's go!

Part One: Getting Started with PowerPoint RT 2013

Chapter 1: First Things First - Supported Devices, Keyboard Covers, and Other Accessories

Before we dive right in, there are a couple of things we'll need to discuss to make sure you're able to get the most out of PowerPoint RT. While this guide is primarily geared toward Surface RT users, Microsoft has licensed the software to a few other hardware companies, which means that you *could* be using any one of these other devices:

- Asus VivoTab RT
- Dell XPS 10
- Samsung Ativ
- Lenovo IdeaPad Yoga (RT)

Office RT will function identically on these other devices, but this section will focus on peripherals you'll want to have for the Surface.

> **Note: Microsoft has released two different versions of the Surface tablet, one labeled Surface RT and one labeled Surface Pro. Since the Surface Pro is essentially a full-fledged computer shoved into a tablet form factor, they do not include <u>any</u> version of Office with it. Office RT is, in fact, a specially coded version of the software meant to be used with what's called ARM processors – chips used primarily in mobile devices. The Surface Pro uses standard X86 chips, which makes it 100% incompatible with Office RT. Long story short: if you bought a Surface Pro, you'll have to buy your own copy of PowerPoint, which will have a slightly different set of features than the version discussed in this guide.*

Covers –

While the Surface RT doesn't automatically ship with a keyboard, Microsoft has engineered two different, equally elegant solutions: the 'touch' cover and the 'type' cover:

The touch cover is not really a keyboard, at least not exactly. It's an incredibly thin, touch-sensitive mat, with a keyboard layout. Completely flat to the touch, typing on it can take a little getting used to. The type cover is more akin to a regular keyboard – the keys have a fair bit of 'travel', which means they move when you press down.

Either solution is perfectly suitable, depending on your preferences, but we highly recommend picking one up. An on-screen keyboard is fine for web browsing or jotting down small notes, but you're definitely going to need a real keyboard to get anything bigger accomplished. Both of these keyboard covers are available for around $120 – the rest of this guide will assume that you've got one.

Both of these keyboard covers also come with a built-in trackpad, which functions in the same way that a laptop trackpad does. For those of you that dislike trackpads, we also recommend picking up a USB mouse. Hundreds of them are compatible with the Surface RT, but if compatibility isn't specifically listed on the model you'd like to pick up, check out www.microsoft.com/compatibility to be sure. A whole lot of devices are compatible, even ones you'd *never* think are. Case in point: Apple's Magic Multi-Touch Trackpad works flawlessly, according to the compatibility check:

Apple Magic Multi-Touch Trackpad

MC380LL/A

Available for:

Windows 8   Windows RT   Windows 7   Compatibility status may vary by operatin

Apple

Homepage   Support   Contact

The Magic Trackpad is the first
multi-touch trackpad designed to
work with your Mac desktop ...

Show more...

Model	Status		Community ratin
MC380LL/A	✓	Compatible No Action Required	Compatible : **3** Votes Not compatible : **0** Votes

Give us your vot

Compatible   Not comp

The same goes for printers. While all three of the printers in our office were compatible, it's a good idea to check the website before getting frustrated when you *need* to print a document right away and can't.

Chapter 2: More Than a Slideshow - A Quick PowerPoint Primer

While many of you are probably already familiar with the concept behind the PowerPoint software, we're sure more than a few of you aren't quite sure what or who this program is for. What follows is a quick history of the idea behind PowerPoint, and a preview of what it can do for you. Feel free to skip this section if you're already pretty familiar with presentation software.

Since the dawn of time, people have needed to present ideas and information to other people. The guy who invented the wheel probably had to *explain* the revolutionary concept to his caveman brethren before the idea really took off. And this is how it's been for the majority of our history: someone needs to explain something to other people, so all of the tools at their disposal become *elements* of a presentation. From cave paintings and grunts to a slide projector and a microphone, the concept has stayed the same.

In big business, presentations have always been a good tool. Whether it's a new product rollout, or the quarterly numbers report, a direct presentation to interested parties has always been a better choice than a simple memo. In the halcyon days before the personal computer changed everything, your average presentation included one of these:

Loaded with a bunch of these things:

Often, businesses employed teams of people to create these 'slides' by laying out information alongside hand-made charts. They would then photograph the result, have the film developed and placed into a slide. Sounds like a bit of a pain, doesn't it? It was, and it was also pretty boring.

Enter Microsoft.

The rise (and increasing power) of the home computer changed the concept forever. While people still need to make the same sorts of presentations, the 'slides' are now created (and altered) digitally, making the process far quicker and a lot more reliable.

First released in 1990 as part of the Microsoft Office Suite, PowerPoint quickly came to dominate the presentation software market. Over the years, the software has been refined and retooled for a changing world, taking what once looked like this:

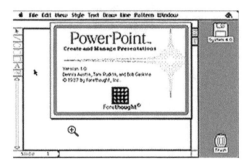

and turning it into this:

Now that Microsoft has unleashed their tablet operating system on the world, they've updated and configured all of their most important Office products to work seamlessly on the Surface and other Windows RT devices. PowerPoint 2013 RT is truly the most powerful version of the software ever created.

The idea, however, is as simple or as complex as you need it to be. To make your presentation, you'll tell a story. Each 'slide' is a part of that story. You'll create as many slides as you like, with transitions between them. Now that computers are powerful enough, you can even add video and/or audio to a slide. You can rearrange and edit your slides at will, using the concept we call non-linear editing. Alongside the slide, you can create notes, visible only to you, to help guide you through a presentation. You can also seamlessly create handouts from your slides to help your audience follow along. Once you've finished creating your presentation, it can be saved, and then played back at any time, in a few different ways.

That's really all there is to it.

If it seems overly complicated, don't worry. We'll show you what you need to know. First, however, let's get your Windows RT tablet updated to fully take advantage of the PowerPoint 2013 RT software.

Chapter 3: Updating/Finalizing Office RT

As you may have already noticed, Windows RT devices shipped with a 'preview' version of all the Office RT apps. Luckily, it's a snap to update it to the final version. According to Microsoft, this update should happen automatically, but that wasn't the case in our experience – we actually attempted an automatic update three times before we gave up. Have no fear, though; Just follow these simple steps to get yourself updated.

> *Note: For some reason, this update doesn't cancel out the original 'preview edition' completely. If you ever have to reset your RT device back to factory defaults, you'll have to go through this update process again. We're not sure why, but it's something you may have to deal with in the future.*

To get started with updating, just bring up the charms bar by swiping right to left. Once you've done that, tap the 'settings' charm:

Once you've done that, you'll be taken to the settings menu, which will look something like this:

To find the update menu, tap 'Change PC Settings'. This will bring up the more advanced menu, which will look like this:

Tap 'Windows Update' to continue. Once there, tap the button labeled 'Check for Updates'. After a few moments, you'll find a list of updates that Microsoft wants to apply. Go ahead and tap 'Install' and let it do its work. Depending on the number of updates that are found, this could take a little while. Trust us; it's worth the hassle to stay updated.

Once you've applied all the updates, your Office apps should no longer be labeled 'Preview' and should look like this on the Home Screen:

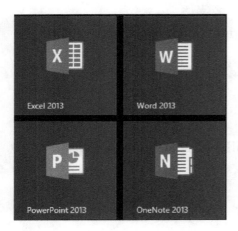

That's all there is to it. We're almost ready to dive right in, but there's one more thing to set up: SkyDrive.

Your Documents in the Cloud: Setting up SkyDrive

Over the last few years, you've probably heard about "The Cloud" and its impact on computing. If you don't know any better, it sounds sort of scary and complicated. Rest assured that it's not. "The Cloud" is really just a buzzword – it's shorthand for online storage and nothing more. How does this relate to your Windows RT tablet?

If you're like most people, you probably have a few internet-connected devices lying around. You might use your desktop computer for some things, while other tasks are relegated to your smart phone or tablet. All these different gadgets are great for getting stuff done, except in one crucial way: how do you get your stuff from one device to another? How do you keep everything organized and up to date? Microsoft's answer to that is SkyDrive, and it's a great solution.

Microsoft has included 10 GB of SkyDrive cloud storage with every Surface tablet, while users of the other Windows tablets we discussed earlier will only have the 7 GB that comes for free. Users of cloud storage services like Dropbox or iCloud will be familiar with the concept behind Microsoft's SkyDrive, but the company's take on it is a little bit different, especially for Windows RT tablets.

Basically, SkyDrive is a folder (or group of folders) stored on the Internet, but accessible only to you and your devices. Copying a file from your computer to SkyDrive will make the file available instantaneously across all of your other SkyDrive-enabled devices. Setting up SkyDrive on your PC is crucial, especially if you use Office on devices other than your Windows RT tablet.

For example, let's say you've created a presentation on your PC. You're sitting in the living room, watching television, when you suddenly remember a point or two that you've forgotten to include. You can just pull the same file up on your Surface tablet and edit it without having to trudge back to your home office. The changes you make from the living room will automatically be applied to the file on your PC.

Since this guide will primarily focus on working with PowerPoint RT, perhaps a better example would be creating a presentation on your Windows RT tablet, and then saving it to SkyDrive for later use.

To get started, we'll have to download the SkyDrive application to whichever devices you'd like. In Windows 8 or on your Windows RT tablet, that's as easy as searching for the app in the App Store and downloading it. If you're using another operating system, like OSX, Windows 7, or Windows Vista, it's a little bit more complicated.

To download the application, head over to www.microsoft.com. Once there, you'll notice a search bar in the upper right hand corner. Type 'SkyDrive' in the search bar and click search. The first result will be the SkyDrive app. Click again to download it.

Once it's downloaded, click to open the file and install it. Follow the prompts and enter your Microsoft ID and password in the fields. Make sure it's the same ID you use on your Windows RT device. That's all there is to it. You'll now have a folder on your desktop that looks like this:

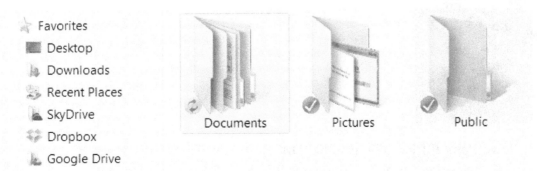

Copy whatever you like to it: documents, music, videos, etc. Whatever you copy will almost instantly appear within the SkyDrive app on your Windows RT tablet:

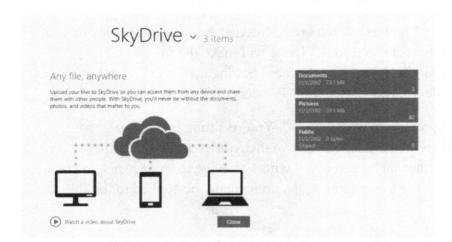

As a special bonus to users of Windows 8, installing SkyDrive will allow you to synchronize the settings of all of your Windows 8 and Windows RT devices. Your tile layout, background, system settings – all of it will match up perfectly if you want it to. Of course, you always have the ability to opt-out of that. For more info on Live Tiles and customization, consult "The Newbies Guide to the Microsoft Surface Tablet", available at www.minutehelpguides.com or from any major bookseller.

Now that you've set up the SkyDrive app, you can share the files on your Surface to it. It's as easy as swiping in the charms bar and tapping Share:

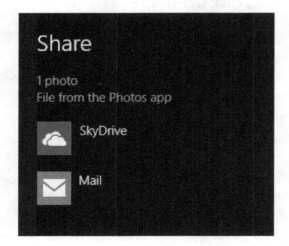

To make it even easier, PowerPoint RT has a built-in SkyDrive solution. Simply tap to save the document you're working on and (after installing it on your Windows RT device) SkyDrive will appear as an option:

But, let's not get ahead of ourselves. In the next section, we'll begin to learn the basics and find our way around the program.

Ready? Let's go!

Chapter 4: Navigating PowerPoint 2013 RT - The Basics

Now that we've gotten through that boring setup stuff, let's dive right in and get started. To do this, we've got to open the program. You can do this one of two ways, and it doesn't matter which one you choose. You can either find the icon on your Start Screen:

Or you can switch your tablet to desktop mode and click the PowerPoint icon on the bottom, which will look like this:

Once you've done that, you'll be presented with PowerPoint's Start Screen. This is where we'll begin every project we undertake. It'll look something like this:

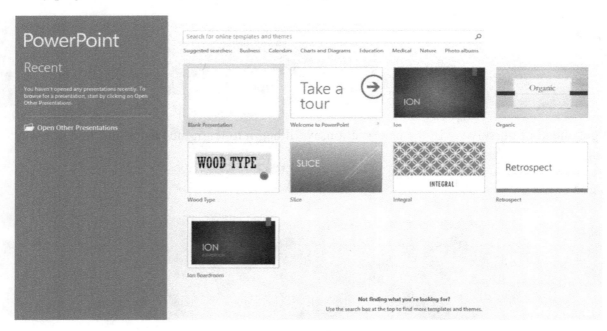

As you can see, you've got a few choices here. The first choice will be highlighted for you, just like the illustration above. Tap here to create a new Blank Presentation. There are also a few templates and a search box near the top used for finding *even more* templates. We'll get to that shortly, but for now, it's a good idea to tap the item labeled 'Take a Tour' and follow it through to get a very quick idea of what we'll be doing.

Once you've done that, go ahead and tap to open a new blank presentation. You'll be taken to a brand new presentation, dubbed Presentation1.

> *The file will keep this name until you've saved it, at which point you can give it any name you like. More on that later.*

You'll notice that there are several components to this view. As illustrated in the screen shot below, there are four main parts to it:

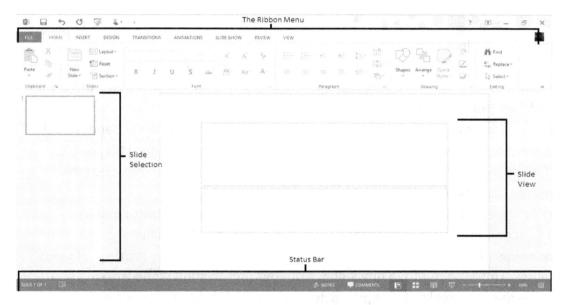

Across the top, you'll find what's referred to as the "Ribbon" menu. If you've used any Microsoft Office program within the last several years, you'll be instantly familiar with it. In case you're not, let's go over it quickly. Don't worry; we'll go into far greater detail a little later.

The Ribbon is, put simply, PowerPoint's menu system. In place of a traditional drop-down menu that you'd expect, Microsoft has instead divided up common tasks and placed them horizontally along the top third of the page. As you can see, there are several different labels toward the top. Each one contains a different set of tasks related to the label. These are called "tabs" and there are nine of them: File, Home, Insert, Design, Transitions, Animations, Slide Show, Review, and View. The view in the above illustration is the "Home" tab, which is what the program defaults to. As you can see, this tab groups together many of the common text elements we'll be working with.

Below and to the left of the Ribbon, you'll find the Slide Selection area. A presentation is made of many different slides, and by clicking a slide in this area, you'll open it for editing in the Slide View area, which takes up the rest of the screen space to the right.

Below that, you'll find what's referred to as the Status Bar. This area contains various bits of information about your project, including (as you can see from the above illustration) the number of the currently selected slide, and the total number of slides in the presentation. To the right of that, you'll find the spelling check icon, and to the right of *that* you'll find icons for opening and closing the notes pane, and for adding or viewing comments, all of which we'll discuss a little later in this guide.

Now, aside from those four main parts, there is one more section of the screen we need to discuss. It's called the Quick-Access Toolbar, and it's located at the very top of your screen, along the left-hand side:

Though this area is often overlooked, using the Quick-Access Toolbar is sometimes the quickest way to get things done in PowerPoint. As you can see, there are several icons. By default, these are (from left to right):

- The minimize/maximize/close button – tapping or clicking here will allow you to make the program take up more (or less) screen space, or also close it entirely. If there have been changes made to the document since the last time it was opened, you'll be asked if you'd like to save any changes before the program closes.
- The save button – allows you to save your document whenever you like with one tap (or click).
- Undo – tapping here will reverse the last thing you did with your presentation. This includes words added, font changes, and any formatting changes you may have done. Tapping (or clicking it) multiple times will continue undoing things one step at a time.
- Redo – tapping or clicking here repeat the last action. This is useful for formatting and/or recreating text boxes and things of that nature, which we'll go over a little later.
- Start From Beginning – tapping here will begin your presentation on-screen, starting (obviously) from the beginning. This is useful for a quick check of your presentation while working on it.
- Touch/Keyboard – this is a toggle. By tapping here, you can switch from a layout optimized for touching with your fingers, or one better suited for use with a keyboard and mouse. The 'touch' portion spreads out the items on the Ribbon, so that they're easier to tap. We'll discuss this further in the next section.

Directly next to the 'Touch/Keyboard' toggle, you'll find another button. By tapping here, you can customize what is displayed on the Quick Access Toolbar. There are dozens of different commands and combinations to choose from. It's all up to you, but in our case, some of the more useful things to add here were:

- Spell Check –tapping this will immediately run through the spelling and grammar check for the whole document.
- Print Preview/Print – obviously only applicable if you've installed a printer to use with your Windows RT tablet.
- Duplicate Slide – this can come in handy when you're creating a longer presentation, with many similar slides that contain only minor changes from the original.

We'll go over a few more of these over the course of the guide, but we'll leave it to you to figure out what works best for your workflow. Many people aren't even aware of this customization option, and thus never miss it.

Now that we've shown you the lay of the land, let's dig a little deeper and learn how to create our own presentations with PowerPoint 2013 RT.

Ready? Let's do this!

Part Two: Using PowerPoint 2013 RT

Chapter 1: The Ribbon Menu - Easier than it Looks

As we discussed in the last section, you'll be spending a lot of time in the Ribbon menu. The Ribbon menu contains within it virtually everything you need to create the best possible PowerPoint presentation. The trick is that it also contains a lot of stuff you'll likely never, ever use. Let's go over each tab, one-by-one, so that we can begin to separate the wheat from the chaff, so to speak.

File – this tab leads you to what Microsoft calls the 'Backstage' view. Backstage is where you'll do everything within the program that isn't focused on the presentation itself. From here, you can save your file, print, share, export, and open previously saved presentations.

Home – as we touched on earlier, Home is basically the nerve center of your presentation. This is where you'll create new slides, change the layout of existing slides, change the look of text, and divide your slides into sections (if necessary) to keep everything organized.

Insert – think of the Insert menu as 'Home' for everything that isn't text. This is where you'll add graphics like text boxes, charts, photos, and Microsoft's patented pieces of SmartArt.

Design – the Design tab is home to the various themes (and variants) that you can apply to your slides. Themes are applied on a project-wide basis, so heading to the Design tab is probably the quickest way to punch up a boring presentation.

Transitions – this tab is the home of all the things that happen *between* the slides of your presentation. Rather than just clicking from one slide to the next, transitions give your presentation a high-end, film or movie edit quality.

Animations – this tab deals with all of the movement that can take place *within* your slides. Text that comes flying in from outside the frame, bouncing sing-a-long style balls, this is where that stuff is kept.

Slide Show – this is where your presentation will be made from. There are quite a few options here, which we'll go over at length later in this guide.

Review – this tab is where you'll review spelling and grammar. If working collaboratively, this is also where you'll add and view comments on the project. Microsoft's 'inking' feature, which we'll discuss a little later in this guide, is also available from here.

View – this is perhaps the most useful tab of all. From here, you can control the current view. By default, you're placed in 'Normal' view, but there are several other options that are useful for different reasons:

- Normal View – used for examining and editing slides on an individual basis. It's helpful to think of this view as the work-mode.
- Outline View – this is used primarily for working with text. It's often helpful to switch to this at first to keep the visual distractions at a minimum.
- Slide View – this view takes the Slide view on the left side of PowerPoint and places it at the forefront. This is useful for rearranging slides, and getting a broad general view of the consistency of the presentation.
- Notes View – this view will show you all of the notes you've created for your slides. We'll talk about notes a little later, as this can be a really helpful tool for presentations.
- Reading View – this view removes everything from the screen in order to focus on the slides individually. It's basically just like a slideshow, but you can quickly stop the flow to edit something whenever you like.

In addition to these views, you'll notice an entirely different view pane labeled 'Master Views'. The Master View is different than any of the others, as it's not about the *content* of your *content*, it's about the style. Clicking on one of the three Master Views will allow you to make changes to the style of your slides, handouts, or notes, all at the same time, without having to change each thing individually. This is incredibly useful for maintaining a consistent visual style, which we'll discuss a little later in this guide.

Chapter 2: Creating a Presentation

Now that we've learned a little bit about the Ribbon, let's dive right in and begin making a sample PowerPoint presentation. To get started, click (or tap) the File tab on the Ribbon and then tap New. From here, we have three basic choices. We can:

- Create a new presentation from scratch
- Use one of the included templates to help us get started
- Search for a template online that strikes our fancy

Normally, we'd recommend starting from scratch. Many of the included templates for Microsoft Office products aren't very useful, aside from very specific cases. Take Microsoft Word for example: the program includes at least three recipe templates, which probably go untouched by 99% of their users. PowerPoint is an exception. There's no greater guarantee that you'll have a consistent visual approach than using something that's been designed by a professional.

When choosing a template, you're given the option to check it out before committing yourself. To do this, just click or tap once on a template. Doing this will open a preview window that will look something like this:

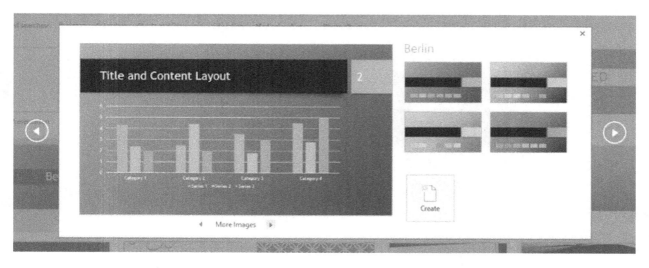

As you can see, there are a lot of options here. In this example, we're looking at a built-in template called Berlin. Notice the four icons on the right hand side. These are the various color schemes included with Berlin. Berlin also includes several different kinds of slides, a few of which are viewable by tapping the button to the right of the 'More Images' label. The arrows all the way to the right and left of the preview will switch to the next template in the list.

Once you've picked a template you like, tap the 'Create' button near the bottom of the preview pane. From there, you'll be taken to your new presentation, which will look like this:

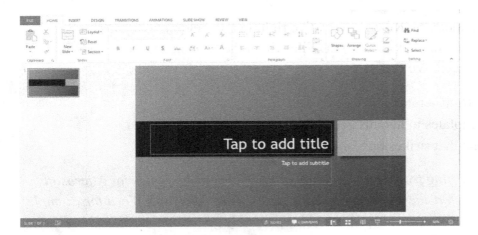

By default, you'll only have one slide in your slide pane. This will generally be what's called a title slide, which is sort of like the book cover of your presentation. Notice that the slide includes text that instructs you about what to put in its place. Double tap or click on 'Tap to add title' to erase that dummy text:

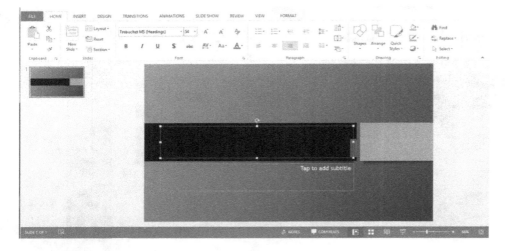

From here, you can replace it with your own. Notice how the text justifies itself to the right-hand side? This kind of thing will happen within every slide, helping to give your presentation a unified look. Once you've entered your title, click anywhere else on the slide to move on.

Next, double click or double tap 'Click to add subtitle' and place any other text you'd like here. If you're not going to use a subtitle, just leave it blank. When you've finished with that, click anywhere else on the slide to move on. Now that you've done these two things, you should be presented with something that looks like this:

Congratulations. You've just created your first slide. Now what?

Well, for starters, let's add some more slides. To do this, make sure you're on the Home tab of the Ribbon menu. You'll see an icon labeled 'New Slide'. Tap the downward facing arrow there to bring up the New Slide menu:

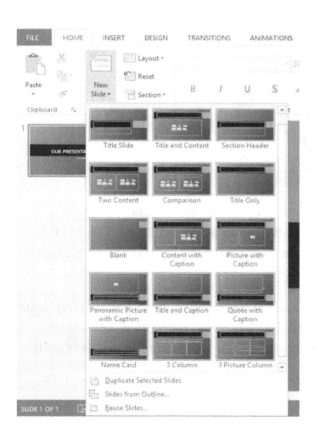

As you can see, you've got a whole lot of choices here. Base your selection on the type of content you'd like to display in the slide. First, we chose a section header, which looks similar to, though not identical to our first title slide:

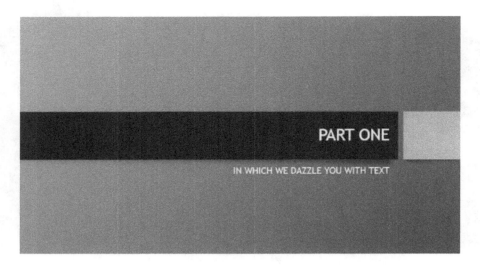

Fill in your desired information in the same way you did before. Once you've done that, choose another slide. For our third slide, we chose 'Quote with Caption', which will look something like this:

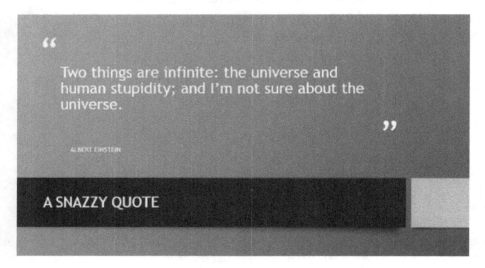

Note that there three places for content in this slide: a quote section (with quotation marks already embedded), an author section below that, and then a caption setting (in black) below that. Though this is a different kind of slide entirely, you can see how it matches the visual cues set forth in the slides that came before it.

Instead of heading for the new slide menu every time you want to create another slide, you can duplicate the current slide to save a little time. To do this, just select a slide, right click to bring up the context menu, and then tap 'Duplicate Slide'. Note that *everything* about the slide will be duplicated, so you'll have to replace any of the text that you'd like to change.

Now that you've got a few simple slides in your project, let's talk about a few things that you'll soon need to know. First up, rearranging.

Once you've created several different slides, you'll probably want to change their order at some point. Thankfully, this is a super easy task. To change the order of your slides, just select the slide you'd like to change in the slide pane on the left hand side and then drag it with either your finger or trackpad to where you'd like it to be.

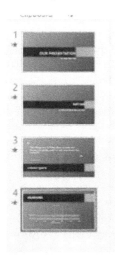

You might also want to remove a slide from your presentation. There are a couple of ways to go about this. First, you can simply delete it by selecting the slide and right clicking to bring up the context menu and tapping the Delete Slide menu item.

> *Remember that you can undo what you've done by tapping the undo icon located on the Quick-Access Toolbar if you accidentally delete something you need.*

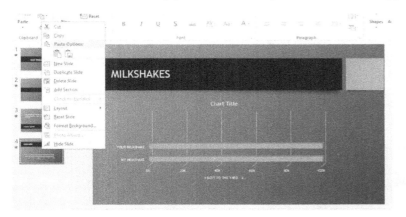

If you're looking for a less permanent solution, you can also hide a given slide. To do this, just right click to bring up the context menu and tap the Hide Slide menu item. Your slide will remain where it is, but it will not be part of your presentation while it's hidden. This has a lot of advantages; you can hide a slide that might not be relevant to your audience, but bring it back if the situation calls for it.

While you're busy making your slides, you might find yourself thinking of information that, though it won't fit on a slide, might be useful to have during your presentation. Whether you plan to include this information in the oral part of your presentation, or whether you'd just like to have the info available, PowerPoint includes a feature to keep track of this stuff: Notes.

Along the bottom of your screen, you'll notice a toolbar with 'Notes' smack dab in the middle of it:

To add a note to a slide, just select it from the slide selection pane and then tap the Notes icon at bottom of the screen. A section along the bottom of the selected slide will come into view. Type anything you like here – it's not part of the presentation; nobody will see it but you. When it comes time to present your PowerPoint project, you'll see the notes alongside the slide in your personal presenter view, which will look like this:

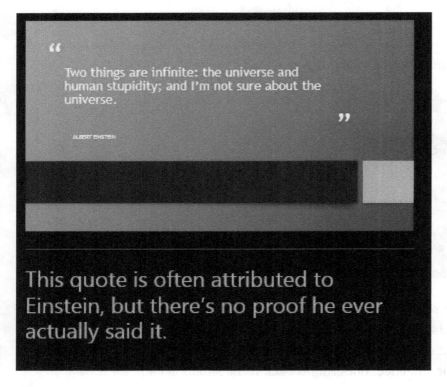

Your viewers will see only the slide on the top, while you will also see any notes you've added. Pretty cool, huh?

Chapter 3: SmartArt and Photos

Now that we've learned how to create some slides for our presentation, let's dig a little deeper and start adding some other types of content. There are several ways to go about this, but let's start with the easiest.

Many of the various kinds of slides are already set up to utilize different kinds of content. To add non-text content to a slide, tap the Add Slide arrow on the Home view of the Ribbon and choose a slide that has the word 'Content' somewhere in its label. For this example, we chose 'Title and Content':

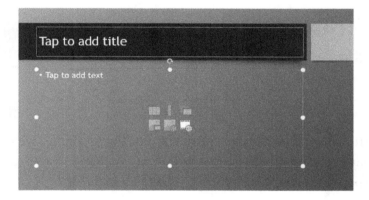

As you can see, the slide is set up in much the same way as our previous slides, with the exception of the bottom portion, where you can see six semi-transparent icons. These icons represent the different types of content that can be placed in that spot, which are:

- Table – often imported from an Excel spreadsheet.
- Chart – this includes several different kinds of visual charts and graphs, sometimes filled with information from an Excel spreadsheet.
- SmartArt – this includes items that show relationships, but aren't necessarily in chart form. Things like pyramids, honeycombs, hierarchies, etc.
- Pictures – this acts as a shortcut to pictures on your tablet, or on your SkyDrive cloud storage
- Online Pictures – a handy shortcut to a Bing image search, as well as clipart stored on Microsoft.com. This is searchable, and more robust than you'd think.
- Videos – either online, or within your personal storage.

For this example, let's add a SmartArt item. To do that, just tap the SmartArt icon within the slide to bring up the SmartArt menu. Once you do that, you'll be presented with this pop-up menu:

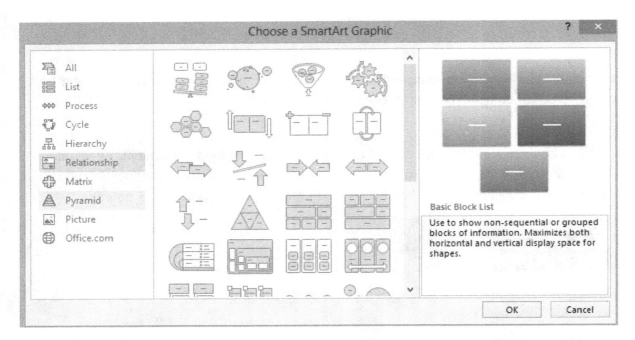

From here, you can see all of the available SmartArt, categorized for easy retrieval. For this example, we chose the 'Counterbalance Arrows'. Note that clicking or tapping on an item will bring up the description for that item on the bottom right of the pop-up menu. Once you've selected a piece of SmartArt, click or tap the OK button.

Once you've done that, your SmartArt will appear in your slide:

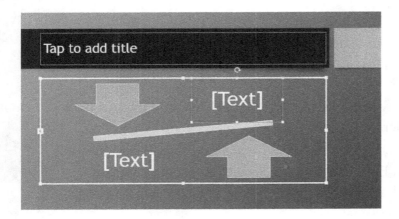

From here, you can resize the item, and add text wherever you like. Add a title, and you've just created a slide using SmartArt:

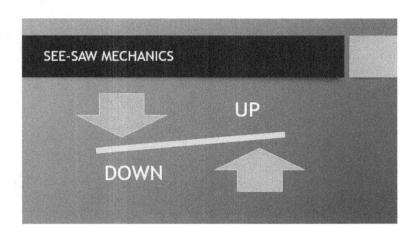

Removing an item from the slide is simple. Simply double-tap or click on it until it's open for editing. Once you've done that, just tap the delete key. The area will revert back to the content options view that it had before.

To add a photo in a content box, just tap one of the photo icons (either web or local) to bring up the Insert Pictures pop-up box:

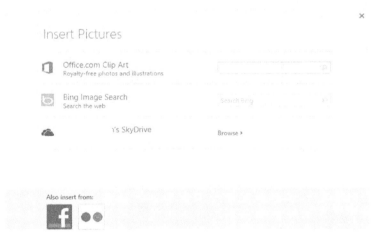

As you can see from the above illustration, you'll be presented with a couple of search boxes. The first will search Microsoft's own collection of clip-art and stock photographs. The second will search the web for photos that can be used. If you've set up SkyDrive, you can browse for any photos you've saved to it. Additionally, you can use photos from your Facebook or Flickr accounts.

For this example, we searched for the phrase "See Saw" in Bing. We were given an extensive visual list of results, chose one, and then tapped OK, which added the photo to our slide instantly:

SEE-SAW MECHANICS

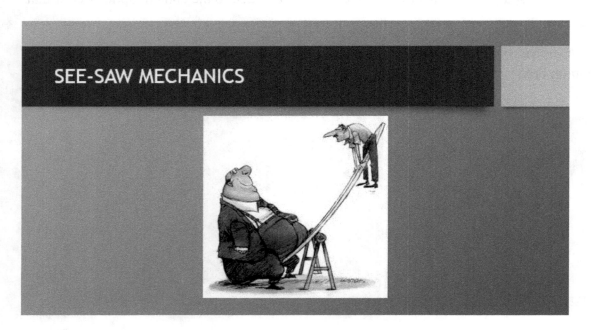

That's all there is to it. You can now add different types of visual content to your presentation.

Chapter 4: Working with Audio and Video

Now that we've got text and pictures covered, you might think we've done all we can do with our slides, right? Not even close. We can also add multimedia files to any slide we like.

This works in the same way as SmartArt and photos, but it can be a little more complex once you get into it. Let's start with audio.

If you recall our discussion about content types from the last section, you'll remember that adding audio to a slide wasn't one of the options listed on the slide's content view. We're assuming that it's only because it's less common a thing to do, but it's really no matter. To add audio, we just have to take one extra step.

Once you've created a content-type slide, go ahead and move to the Insert tab on the Ribbon menu. All the way to the right, you'll find the Add Audio menu:

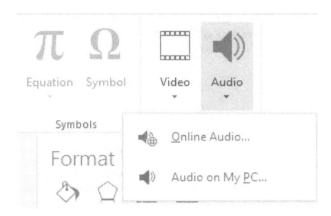

You have two options from here, Online Audio and Audio on my PC. Now, you won't find a Bing search bar under the Online Audio menu, but you will find an Office.com search bar. Search for anything you like, they have a pretty extensive catalog of royalty-free sound clips. Once you've found what you're looking for, tap or click OK to insert it into your slide. Once you've done that, your slide will look something like this:

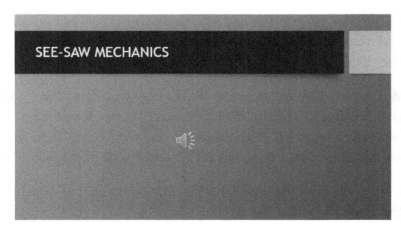

Now, depending on the volume and duration of your audio file, it may not fit perfectly with what you're trying to accomplish. Have no fear, as you can edit virtually everything about your audio file right from the Ribbon.

To edit your audio file, just click on the file's icon until the Audio Tools menu appears on the Ribbon:

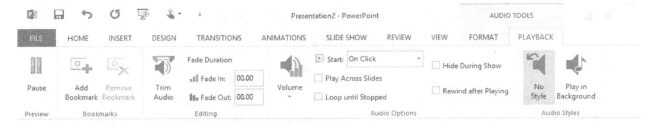

As you can see, there are quite a few options here. For those already familiar with audio editing, you'll recognize the Fade in/Fade Out and Trim Audio commands.

The most often used option here is probably the Trim Audio command. This is exactly what it sounds like: you can take any piece of audio and tell PowerPoint to only play a certain portion of it. It's a lot simpler than it sounds. To get started with trimming audio, just select your audio within the slide and then tap the Trim Audio icon. Once you've done that, you'll be presented with a pop-up window that looks like this:

Notice the two colored markers on either end of the window? These represent the beginning (green) and the end (red) of your audio file. To trim your audio file, just drag the green marker to where you'd like the audio to begin, and then drag the red marker to where you'd like the audio to end. Test out your selection by tapping the play button in the middle. Trimming audio in this way doesn't actually delete anything, so you can change the markers as many times as you like. When you're satisfied, just tap the OK button. That's all there is to it.

A full tutorial on the rest of this stuff is beyond the scope of this guide, but it's not difficult to figure out. Feel free to experiment, and remember: the 'Undo' button is right on the top of the screen!

Video can be added to your slides in a more direct way. You can begin working with video using the content slide method we've already discussed. One thing to keep in mind, however: Microsoft offers no video search and paste method like they do for clipart and audio. If you'd like to use a video, you'll have to already have the video you'd like to use saved to either your Windows RT tablet or your SkyDrive.

To get started with video, just tap the video icon within your content slide. You'll be presented with an explorer window where you can browse for the video file you'd like to

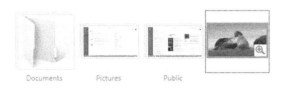

use:

Once you've found your video, tap or click on it to select it and then tap Insert. You'll then be taken back to your slide, which will have a YouTube-like box in the middle of it:

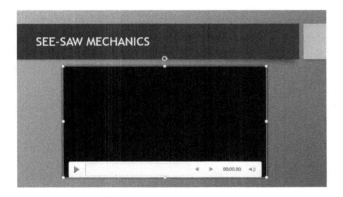

Use the points on the sides to resize your video. You can resize it however you'd like without changing the aspect ratio of the video. Once you've resized the video to your liking, use the Ribbon menu to edit it further:

As you can see, the video menu on the Ribbon is identical to the audio menu we just discussed. Trimming your video works in exactly the same way.

On the right hand side of your screen, next to the slide itself, you'll find another menu:

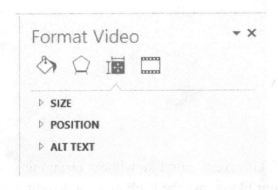

You can use this menu to adjust the video's size, color, brightness, and position to your exact needs.

That's all there is to it.

Chapter 5: Transitions and Animations

Now that we've got a variety of slides in our presentation, we can begin adding a little flourish to them. Using Transitions and Animations is a great way to add a little pizazz to your PowerPoint work, so let's spend a moment to figure out how to get this done, shall we?

Transitions – a Transition is, to put it simply, the stuff that happens *between* your slides. Just like in your favorite movies and television shows, PowerPoint doesn't need to just jump from slide to slide. Adding a transition can help convey movement and change in a way that jumping from slide to slide can't.

To get started with transitions, select the first slide by tapping it in the slide selection pane, and then tap the Transitions tab on the Ribbon menu. You'll be greeted with a Ribbon menu that looks like this:

As you can see, there are quite a few options here. Any Transition you select will be immediately applied to the slide you've selected. You can preview the Transition by tapping the preview button on the left. While you have dozens of options for which transition to choose, it's a good idea to stay as consistent as possible. To apply a Transition to *every* slide in your presentation, all you have to do is double-click (or double-tap) the 'Apply to All' icon on the Ribbon. This can save you a lot of time, especially if your presentation is large.

You can also add audio effects to your transitions. To do this, just tap the drop-down arrow next to 'Sound' on the Transitions Ribbon. Again, you have dozens of options to choose from, and you can apply the sound to every slide by double-clicking 'Apply to all'.

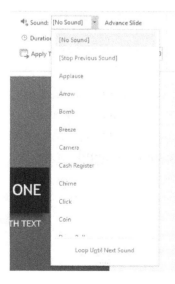

Animations – closely related to Transitions, Animations are simply transitions *within* a slide. Remember how each slide generally has a few different elements? Each one of those elements can be animated, making the individual elements of a slide move into (or out of) frame. To get started with Animations, select a slide and then tap the Animations tab on the Ribbon menu.

Once you've done that, you'll be presented with a Ribbon menu that looks similar to the Transitions menu we just discussed.

At this point, go ahead and select an element of your slide by clicking it. As you can see below, our slide has three different elements, all of which can be animated on an individual basis.

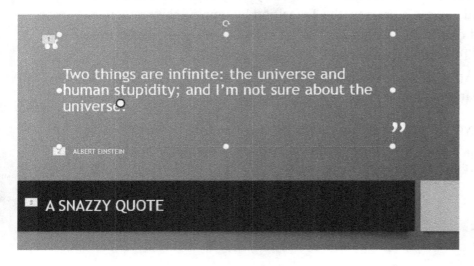

Feel free to experiment with different animations. Once you've found what you're looking for, head to the right side of the Ribbon menu, where you'll see an icon labeled 'Start'. Select the behavior you'd like from the dropdown menu. You can set these animations to begin the moment the slide begins, or set it to wait for you to click before the slide comes to life. We'll discuss this a little more in depth in the next section of this guide.

Part Three: Getting More Out of PowerPoint 2013 RT

Now that we've learned all about creating a PowerPoint presentation, it's time to send it out into the world. Let's dig a little deeper and learn how to record our presentation, export it to various formats, and share it with the world.

Chapter 1: Recording and Exporting

We've got a bunch of slides, full of great content, beautiful transitions, and eye-catching animations. Now what? The final step on the road to a finished PowerPoint presentation is recording.

To begin recording your PowerPoint presentation, tap the Slide Show tab on the Ribbon menu. You'll be presented with the Slide Show Ribbon, which looks like this:

What we're going to do is record our actions alongside the presentation, timing it to make sure it moves at a pace we're comfortable with. To begin this process, just tap the "Record Slide Show" button on the Ribbon.

Once you've done that, you'll be presented with a pop-up box:

Tap "Start Recording" when you're ready to begin. You'll be presented with your Slides, starting with the first one in the project. In the upper left hand corner, you'll see a timer:

Now, using the forward arrow key on your keyboard, you can move through the slides at your pace. If you have a speech prepared to go along with your PowerPoint, it's a good idea to read it aloud at the same time. Remember that any animations in your slides will usually begin when you've tapped the arrow key *each time*. You'll also want to press play on any video or audio files that aren't set to automatically play. Once you've finished the last slide, you'll be asked to save your timing:

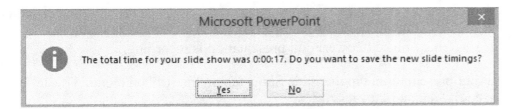

Tap yes to save it. You can re-record at any time if you'd like to change anything.

Now that you've recorded your PowerPoint presentation, you can actually export it to video for viewing on televisions, DVDs, or the web. The video will be exactly as long as the recording you've made. To export your video, just tap the File tab on the Ribbon menu to head to the backstage view. Once you're there, tap the menu item labeled Export:

As you can see, you have a few options. Tapping 'Create PDF' will create a PDF of all of your slides, viewable on virtually every computer. Tapping Package Presentation for CD will copy the presentation, including any audio or video, to a CD for easy retrieval. Tapping 'Create Handouts' will create printer-friendly versions of every slide in your presentation, usually with at least two slides per page, which helps save space.

Creating a video of your project is just as easy. Just tap 'Create a Video' to get started. From there, you'll be greeted with the video menu:

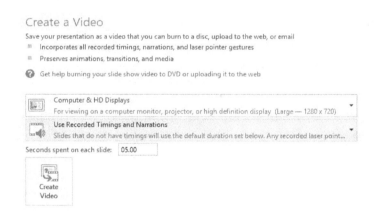

Create a Video

Save your presentation as a video that you can burn to a disc, upload to the web, or email

- Incorporates all recorded timings, narrations, and laser pointer gestures
- Preserves animations, transitions, and media

? Get help burning your slide show video to DVD or uploading it to the web

Computer & HD Displays
For viewing on a computer monitor, projector, or high definition display (Large — 1280 x 720)

Use Recorded Timings and Narrations
Slides that do not have timings will use the default duration set below. Any recorded laser point...

Seconds spent on each slide: 05.00

Create
Video

As you can see, you have the option to use your recorded timings for the video, though you can also just set a default time that each slide will display. Choose the quality you'd like for your video (HD or non HD quality) and then tap Create Video. Save the resulting file wherever you like. You can upload the resulting video to any video-sharing service you like, such as YouTube, Vimeo, etc.

Chapter 2: Sharing and Presenting

Now that we've learned how to record and export our PowerPoint presentation, let's take a quick moment to discuss our options for sharing and presenting our work. Head to the backstage view and tap the item labeled Share to get started.

There are several ways to share your presentation with other people. First, you can invite people to view your presentation. To do this, click on the 'Invite People' menu item. If you haven't yet, you'll need to save your document to SkyDrive before getting this set up:

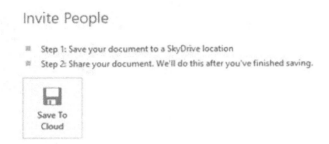

Just tap the 'Save to Cloud' icon to get started, and save the document like you ordinarily would. Once you've done that, you'll be taken to a page that will allow you to enter the names of your contacts, or standard email addresses of people you'd like to share the presentation with.

By default, these people will be able to edit your document, make changes, and download it to their home computers. If you'd like to restrict their access to read-only, change the drop-down menu on the right side of the screen to read 'Can View' rather than 'Can Edit':

Below this, you're given space to enter a message for your recipients. Once you've entered all of that information, just click the 'Share' icon to send a link to everyone on your list:

To bypass all that email sending, you can simply head to the next menu item. Labeled 'Get a Sharing Link,' clicking here will allow you to copy the URL (Internet address) where the file is located. Anyone you give this URL to will be able to access the document.

You're actually given two different links: one for people to view the document, and another for people to edit the document.

If all of the options we've just discussed aren't quite enough for you, Microsoft has also included automatic sharing to your social networks as a choice. Of course, you'll need to have connected your Windows RT tablet to your social networks to use this feature. If you've done that already, it's a snap to share this way. Just click the menu item labeled 'Post to Social Networks'. Once you've done that, you'll be presented with a menu that looks something like this:

As you can see, all of your connected social networks will appear with a checkmark next to them by default. If you'd only like to share to one social network, just tap the checkmark to remove it from the list. Much like the 'Share' option, you're given an option to allow people to edit (or just view) the document, as well as some space to add a message. Bear in mind that Twitter has a 140 character limit, so do your best to not be overly verbose.

Once you've made your selections, tap the icon labeled 'Post' at the bottom. Almost instantaneously, your presentation will appear as a clickable item on the selected social network(s).

Chapter 3: Presenting, Projectors and Secondary Displays

We've talked a lot about making PowerPoint presentations over the course of this guide, usually under the assumption that the actual *playing* of your PowerPoint files would be taken care of at some later date by someone experienced with the equipment necessary to make a presentation to a waiting audience. The truth is, your Surface tablet and a couple of accessories are all you really need to cut out the middle man and present your own PowerPoint presentations in a completely professional way.

There are three main ways that a PowerPoint presentation can be made using your Windows RT device. The first, most obvious, probably least effective way is just by using the tablet's screen. While this can work for one-on-one or small groups, it's not very practical for anything larger. To do this, just tap the 'Play Slideshow' icon on the Quick-Access Toolbar.

The second way is by using an external monitor or television. Depending on the size of your secondary display, this can work out well, affording you the luxury of the presentation view we discussed earlier:

To present this way, you'll need to press ALT-FN-F5 on your keyboard.

To present this way, you'll also need to purchase an adapter of some kind. This is, as they say, how they get you.

Microsoft sells two different video adapters for the Surface RT. Each one is $39.99, and they both do the same thing:

Surface VGA Adapter
$39.99
* Designed exclusively for
  Surface with Windows RT
* Connects to VGA-compatible
  displays
* Share pictures, videos, and
  big ideas

Surface HD Digital AV
Adapter
$39.99
* Designed exclusively for
  Surface with Windows RT
* Connects to HDMI-
  compatible displays
* Stream movies, play games,
  watch videos

If you'd like to connect a standard VGA monitor (or non-HD television), the Surface VGA adapter is what you're looking for. If you're going to connect to an HDTV-type device, you would think that the Surface HD Digital AV Adapter is the one you would buy. You'd be *wrong*.

The Surface RT tablet actually comes with HDMI built in. It's the small port on the side by the USB ports. It doesn't look like HDMI because it's Micro-HDMI – the same connection in a smaller package. All you really need to purchase to make an HDMI connect is a Micro-HDMI to HDMI cable, which can be purchased anywhere for less than 5 bucks:

Fosmon HDMI to Micro HDMI Cable (6 Feet)
by Fosmon Technology
★★★★☆ ☑ (555 customer reviews)

List Price: ~~$11.15~~
Price: $4.89
You Save: $6.26 (56%)

In Stock.
Ships from and sold by CobraCables/CableForge.

8 new from $2.02   2 used from $2.99   2 refurbished from $2.99

The third way to use your Surface RT device to make a presentation is by connecting a projector to the device. This is arguably the best solution for larger presentations, but—like the other options – it does come with its own pitfalls.

The first thing you'll need to consider is price. If you've got an unlimited corporate expense account, you're in luck! Some of these devices can be *wildly* expensive. The trick is that they don't necessarily look or act a whole lot different than their more reasonably priced counterparts.

There are three basic types of projectors that you're likely to encounter while shopping around: Pico Projectors, Business Projectors, and Home Theatre Projectors. Business-class projectors are made for this type of application, but they can run anywhere from $800 to thousands. Home Theatre projectors are often a little bit cheaper, but they're designed for full-motion video and require a lot more setup than the others.

Your best bet is to research the emerging Pico Projector market. Pico projectors are generally compact, sleek little machines that are meant to be portable. You can throw a Pico projector into your laptop bag and carry it with you wherever you go. They can be had from around $150 on up to several hundred or more. You'll need a room that's capable of getting pretty dark, however, as most portable projectors don't really have the powerful light bulbs needed for display in lighted rooms.

Optoma PK120, nHD, 18 LED Lumens, Pico Pocket Projector
by Optoma
★★★★☆ ☑ (26 customer reviews)

List Price: $199.00
Price: $149.99 & FREE Shipping. Details
You Save: $49.01 (25%)

In Stock.
Ships from and sold by Amazon.com. Gift-wrap available.

Want it tomorrow, March 22? Order within 3 hrs 5 mins, and choose One-Day Shippi

27 new   11 used from $124.73

While new Pico projectors are released pretty consistently, at the time of this writing, we found the Optoma PK120 to be a pretty good option. We were able to find it for $149.99 from several different stores.

One great advantage of a projector like this one is the included MicroSD slot. You can actually copy your PowerPoint file to a MicroSD card and play it automatically through the PK120 without using a computer at all. This little device will even support video files copied directly to MicroSD. If you hadn't already guessed, this can come in very handy in case of a computer emergency.

Keep in mind, no matter which projector you pick up, it's a good idea to head to the Microsoft Compatibility Center (discussed near the beginning of this guide) to make sure everything will work with your Windows RT device.

Good Luck!

Chapter 4: Making Better PowerPoint Presentations

Over the course of this guide, we've shown you how to create a PowerPoint presentation. Now that we've learned quite a bit about the *mechanics* of the program, let's take some time to talk about the *art* behind it.

If you've ever been on the receiving end of a bad PowerPoint presentation, you're already well aware of how truly terrible (and terrifying!) it can be. Boring slides, weird colors, awkward transitions, and information packed so tight on the screen that even Superman couldn't digest the idea in the timeframe given. You may not know *exactly* why a given presentation sucks, you just know that it does, and you don't want all of your carefully planned out PowerPoint work to go to waste, do you? Based on our (completely unscientific) survey of colleagues and friends, we've come up with what we think is a good starting point.

Easy on the Text

PowerPoint presentations exist to give information to the viewer. That said, cramming every word you can onto a slide is generally not the way to go about it. Unless you're using direct quotes, stick to things that can fit in a bullet point.

- While we're on the subject, using bullet points is a *great* way to separate information into manageable chunks.

Now, just because you've kept the text light doesn't mean you're out of the woods yet. Make sure that your text is in a readable, large (but not overly large) font. Coloring your text red or purple to 'brighten up the page' is seldom a good idea for your audience.

Use Simple Transitions

While PowerPoint offers a huge range of transitions, it's always a good idea to be judicious with them. Not every word needs its own custom wipe or dissolve. Too much visual trickery can be a big distraction, and distraction is your enemy.

Charts, Graphs, and Diagrams are your Friends

Whoever said that a picture is worth a thousand words was, in all likelihood, not referring to stock pieces of clipart. A majority of your images should be informational and *not* scenery. A well-placed pie chart can explain a difficult concept in 5 seconds, while a block of text can half-explain it in an entire minute.

Don't be a Robot

Even if your PowerPoint is visually perfect, your *personal* presentation shouldn't be neglected. If you're speaking along with your presentation, the last thing you should do is parrot the information in your

PowerPoint. Think of yourself as a companion piece to the presentation, and practice your own spin before doing it in front of an audience.

Charts and diagrams are great places to expound on an idea. Your audience can see the facts, and then hear a related anecdote from your mouth. Studies have shown time and time again that this combination can be *ridiculously* effective when it comes to information retention, which is the entire point of the presentation, right? Use the Notes feature we discussed earlier if at all possible. That'll help you keep it together.

For God's Sake, Proofread

Even the most attentive person is bound to make a proofing error at some point. It's nothing to be ashamed of, but if you let that slipup make its way into your final presentation, someone is going to notice, and when they do, they'll stop retaining your information.

It's a good idea to proofread twice, and then get a second pair of eyes to do the same. This applies not just to spelling and grammar, but also to any facts or figures you've used in your presentation. Nothing stops a presentation dead like someone who feels the need to stop you and argue about the truth of a particular point.

Practice Makes Perfect

There's a leisure activity that's growing in popularity the world over. It's called PowerPoint Karaoke. The idea is as simple as it is hilarious. A group of people, usually in a bar, will take turns giving a PowerPoint presentation. The 'Karaoke' part of the equation is that none of them have any idea what the presentation will be before they start giving it. It's often very funny, and always an adrenaline rush for the participants. It's also, we promise you, the exact opposite of what you want to happen during any *real* PowerPoint presentation.

Avoiding your own PowerPoint Karaoke is simple. You've got to learn the material inside-out before giving your presentation. The last thing you want is an adrenaline pumping surprise.

PowerPoint can be a resource-intensive application. It's always a good idea to do a trial run on a presentation, using the same equipment, before the real thing. A computer crash will kill any momentum you've created, and it'll be next to impossible to get things back on track before your audience has checked out.

This is doubly important if you've loaded your presentation with multimedia of any sort: videos, audio, large pictures, all of these things can use up your computer's available memory a lot faster than you'd think, even in today's high-tech world. After all, even the guy running the slide projector in the 70s knew it was a good idea to keep an extra light bulb handy.

Conclusion

Well, that's about it. You should be well on your way to mastering PowerPoint 2013 RT. You should now be able to navigate your way around, create some beautiful presentations, and share them with the world. You can take a project from a blank slate to a finished masterpiece. You can take a template and truly make it your own. We've shown you the essentials, but more importantly, we've tried to instill in you the confidence to tackle any kind of presentation task that might come your way tomorrow, while allowing you to get things done today.

We sincerely hope you've enjoyed reading this guide as much as we've enjoyed writing it. We're sure that you'll be getting plenty of use out of Office RT 2013 on your Windows RT tablet for years to come.

Thanks for reading!

About Minute Help Press

Minute Help Press is building a library of books for people with only minutes to spare. Follow @minutehelp on Twitter to receive the latest information about free and paid publications from Minute Help Press, or visit minutehelpguides.com.